BRITAIN IN OLD PHOTOGRAPHS

THE BOROUGHS OF
WANDSWORTH &
BATTERSEA AT WAR

PATRICK LOOBEY & JON MILLS

LONDON BOROUGH OF WANDSWORTH

SUTTON PUBLISHING

Sutton Publishing Limited
Phoenix Mill · Thrupp · Stroud
Gloucestershire · GL5 2BU

First published 1996

Title page illustration: Peter Derek
Willeringhaus (*see* page 37).

British Library Cataloguing in Publication Data
A catalogue record for this book is available from the
British Library.

ISBN 0-7509-0944-7

Typeset in 10/12 Perpetua.
Typesetting and origination by
Sutton Publishing Limited.
Printed in Great Britain by
Ebenezer Baylis, Worcester.

Jon Mills, born in Balham, lived in Putney for thirty-five years. Educated at Emanuel School at Clapham
Junction he subsequently qualified as a librarian and worked for Wandsworth Libraries until 1980. Since
that date he has specialised in information work for chartered surveyors and is currently employed as an
information manager for a large central London firm. His interest in the Home Front of the Second
World War grew out of an enthusiasm for military history which was sparked by tales of his grandfather
who served as an air raid warden in Wandsworth throughout the war, and his father who served in the
Wandsworth Battalion of the Home Guard. He started collecting insignia of the Home Front some twenty
years ago and his collection has expanded to include memorabilia of all aspects of the civilian war. During
his time with Wandsworth Libraries he researched the history of the borough in the war which was
published in 1989, and has subsequently published a book on the uniforms of Civil Defence in the period.
From 1970 until 1989 he served with the local Territorial Army infantry unit based in Balham, setting up
a museum for them which was opened in 1981. Jon has supplied some of the technical information for
this book.

Patrick Loobey, born 1947, has lived most of that time in Wandsworth and joined the Wandsworth
Historical Society in 1969. He has served on its archaeological, management and publishing committees
and was chairman of the society from 1991 to 1994. Since 1993, Patrick has compiled a series of
photographic books that cover Wandsworth and Battersea. Having collected Edwardian postcards of
Wandsworth Borough and surrounding districts for over twenty years, he has a wide-ranging collection of
more than 20,000 cards encompassing many local roads and subjects.

HMS *Bulldog*. The people of Battersea raised
£½ million during Warship Week, March 1942,
and adopted this destroyer.

CONTENTS

ACKNOWLEDGEMENTS

I must thank the following for their assistance in the preparation of this book: Meryl Jones, Principal Librarian-Development Officer at Wandsworth Libraries, for believing in this publication. Tony Shaw, Wandsworth Local History Librarian, for making the collection of photographs available. Susan Barber, Assistant Curator of Wandsworth Museum, for making the collection of wartime material accessible. Bob Jenner, for sharing his vast knowledge of wartime Wandsworth. Joan Morgan of the Mayfield Association. William Mackett, former resident of 25 Mantua Street, Battersea. Joan White, former resident of 12 Corunna Road, Streatham. Evelyn and Margaret Hunt, ex-Mayfield School, residents of Amerland Road, Wandsworth. Paul McCue, for the loan of photographs of Corporal Foster and information. M. Bailey, Wandsworth Rifle Club. Peter White, former member of the Tooting Home Guard. Mrs Newberry, widow of John Newberry RAF, DFC. Hugh Steeper Ltd, for permission to reproduce the photograph on page 17. John Warburton, for permission to reproduce the photograph on page 108. Robert Armstrong, whose mother served for five years in the National Fire Service.

Books and periodicals invaluable as sources: A. Shaw & J. Mills, *We Served – Wartime Wandsworth and Battersea*, Wandsworth Libraries, 1989. *Wandsworth Official Guide*, Wandsworth Council, 1948. Report on the repair of war damage in Battersea, Battersea Borough Council, 1948. 'Streatham's 41' (Flying bombs on Streatham), Anonymous, 1945. Patrick Loobey, *Flights of Fancy – Aviation Pioneers in Wandsworth and Battersea*, Wandsworth Libraries, 1981. *Morgans at War*, Morgan Crucible Co. Ltd., 1946. *Marching to War 1933–1939, Illustrated London News*, Bracken Books, 1989. *Streatham News*, 1939–45. *Clapham Observer*, 1939–45. *Wandsworth Borough News*, 1939–47. *South Western Star*, 1939–45.

Thanks must be made to the following individuals and organisations that have allowed me to copy their photographs. Photograph credits (page numbers: T=Top, L=Lower): Robert Armstrong, 64; Brandlehow School, 95L, 96; Pamela Cade, 100L, 101; Mrs Collen, 48T; D. Foster, via Paul McCue, 22; Mrs Gamble, 109; Bob Jenner, 53L; Mrs Leserve, 112, 113T; Patrick Loobey, 7, 8L, 9, 10, 11, 12, 13, 14, 15, 16, 17, 18, 19T, 20L, 21, 23, 24, 50, 51, 54L, 74L, 97L, 103, 110, 111L, 119L, 124, 125L, 126L, 127, 128; Jon Mills, 35, 37T, 38, 46T, 53T, 60L, 61L, 62T, 65L, 66T, 75, 77, 78, 81L, 83L, 90, 93, 97T, 100T; Mrs Newberry, 102; Tom Ridgeway, Battersea Park, 84, 85, 87, 88L, 89T; Mrs Taylor, 118L, 119T; John Tatchell, 62L, 111T; Derek Vidler, 30, 120T; Wandsworth Borough Rifle Club, 8T; Wandsworth Historical Society, 92L; Wandsworth Local History Library, Lavender Hill, 19L, 20T, 26, 27, 28, 29, 31, 32, 33, 34, 36, 37L, 46L, 47, 49, 52, 54T, 55, 56, 57, 58, 59, 60T, 61T, 63, 66L, 70, 71, 72, 73, 74T, 76, 79, 82L, 83T, 86, 88T, 91L, 92, 94, 98T, 99, 106, 115L, 117L, 122T, 123, 125T, 126; Wandsworth Museum, Court House, Garratt Lane, 25, 39, 40, 41, 42, 43, 44, 45, 48L, 65T, 67, 68, 69, 80, 81T, 82T, 89L, 91T, 95T, 98L, 104, 105, 116, 117T, 118T, 120L, 121, 122L; John Warburton, 108; 'Streatham's 41' kindly loaned by Derek Vidler, 107, 113L, 114, 115T.

Patrick Loobey, 1996

INTRODUCTION

On the day war broke out, the staff of the *Streatham News* pinned a quotation to the office wall and printed it in their edition of 11 May 1945, 'The spirit of the British nation enables it to carry through to victory any struggle it once enters upon, no matter how long the struggle may last or however great the sacrifice that may be necessary or whatever the means to be employed; and all this although the actual equipment at hand may be utterly inadequate when compared with that of any other nation', Adolf Hitler, *Mein Kampf*, 1924.

The photographs within these pages depict some of the struggles and sacrifices undergone by the people of Wandsworth and Battersea during the First and Second World Wars. In 1939 the combined population of these two boroughs was nearly half a million, allowing for the evacuation of mothers and children in that year and for those serving in the Forces. However, the population was still large enough that the stories of everyone who lived in Wandsworth and Battersea could not be told here – they would overwhelm this book. The incidents recorded here have also depended on the availability of photographs, which were mainly of an official nature during the Second World War. Film for private use was not easy to acquire and it is often difficult persuading people that photographs in family albums are of interest and worth sharing. I would be pleased if anyone was to contact me with either their wartime memories or photographs of that period – a second volume might develop. P.J. Loobey, 231 Mitcham Lane, Streatham SW16 6PY. Tel 0181 769 0072.

An official book of remembrance, commemorating the 1,301 civilians who died in Wandsworth during the period 1939–45, can be found at the head of the marble staircase in Wandsworth town hall. A list of the 531 civilians who were killed in Battersea is available at the Local History Library, Lavender Hill.

Rolls Royce ambulance, London Auxiliary Ambulance Station (LAAS) at Althorpe Road, off Wandsworth Common, *c.* 1944.

FIRST WORLD WAR

The Putney Volunteers on parade in Chelverton Road, c. 1912. Many of these volunteer battalions were formed throughout Battersea and Wandsworth. Similar to today's Territorial Army, the volunteers had a long tradition – many similar groups were formed and disbanded during the Napoleonic wars and reformed at the end of the nineteenth century, but members of such groups, although willing to serve in an emergency, were probably too old to assist on any battlefront.

The Wandsworth Borough Rifle Club, founded in 1903, bought two disused horse-drawn tramcars for £4 10s to use as their club house, on meadow land by the River Wandle in Earlsfield. The ranges and club grounds were used for training a total of 3,000 troops during the First World War in the use of weapons and even in bridge-building techniques. The two tramcars were sold in 1907 for the same sum they had cost, being replaced by a large, wooden indoor firing range and clubroom, which survives.

During the First World War, the Royal Naval Air Service No. 1 Balloon Training Wing used the grounds of the Roehampton Club, with its headquarters nearby at 331 Upper Richmond Road. No. 2 Training Wing were based in Richmond Park. The RNAS supplied observers, in tethered balloons, as artillery spotters and cadets were trained in ballooning techniques with flights from the Hurlingham Club and from Wandsworth gas works. Cadets of the naval wing of the Royal Flying Corps are seen inflating a balloon at Wandsworth (possibly Wandsworth Common) in 1915.

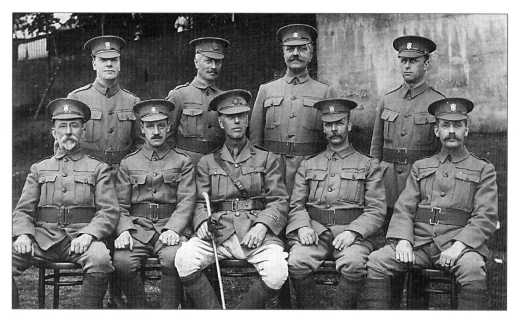

Men of the Wandsworth Volunteer Training Corp, *c.* 1918, these were the First World War equivalent of the Home Guard, consisting of men too old or not medically fit for military service. The corp was renamed as the Wandsworth Volunteer Regiment, with the cap badge incorporating the borough coat of arms.

The Mayor of Wandsworth, Councillor Sir Archibald D. Dawnay, with the 13th Service Battalion of the East Surrey Regiment, the Wandsworth Battalion, leaving for the Western Front in 1915. The battalion distinguished itself on 24 April 1917 by capturing the village of Villers Plouich, ten miles south-west of Cambrai – Corporal Foster of Tooting gaining his Victoria Cross. The village was almost destroyed during the war and was adopted afterwards by Wandsworth, who donated £1,250 in money and goods towards reconstruction, which was completed in 1928.

Many of the volunteer groups were cyclist battalions, but with increasing mechanisation many transport firms would willingly loan their vehicles for training. The upper view is of a lorry from French's garage, Balham High Road, on manoeuvres with the Essex and Suffolk Cyclist Battalion, *c.* 1912. The Streatham Volunteer Corps had their drill hall in Eardley Road. With the start of hostilities, and the consequent addition of many local men, extra facilities were not available locally and the Volunteers are seen at their Whitsun training camp in 1915.

London had twenty-eight air raids during the First World War and both Tooting and Streatham suffered damaged buildings and fatalities. A Zeppelin flew over south London on 24 September 1916, dropping a number of bombs on Streatham which killed thirteen people and injured thirty-three. These views are of the funeral procession, 29 September, of tram conductor Charles Boys and T. Gaymer, the driver of a tram on Streatham Hill which was destroyed. Tramway staff from all over Britain attended the funeral and wreaths were sent from virtually all tram, bus and cab garages.

The use of aluminium in aircraft construction during the war was mainly limited to water tanks for observation balloons and fuel tanks for aircraft. A pioneer in the use of aluminium was Dr Seligman, whose company, the Aluminium Plant and Vessel Co., had works at Point Pleasant, Wandsworth near the River Wandle. The photograph is of food and fuel tanks being produced in the company workshops some time after the war.

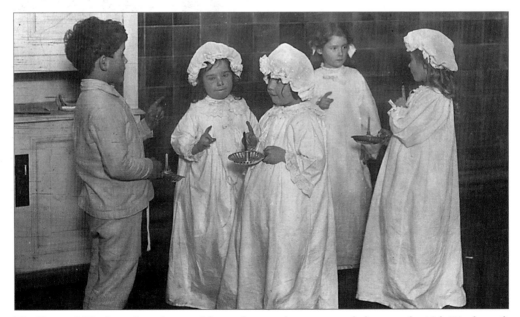

The Mayor of Wandsworth made a special appeal to supply a motor ambulance to the 13th Wandsworth Battalion. This was accomplished in 1915 by a series of collecting events, among which was a grand entertainment given by the children of Streatham secondary training college and Furzedown schools. The picture shows one of the scenes put on by the infants entitled 'The Dance of Good Night'.

The Palladium Autocar Co. moved to Felsham Road, Putney in 1914 manufacturing small private cars and a series of commercial vehicles, lorries and buses which were soon diverted for use in the war effort. In 1918 they were awarded a contract to construct 100 de Havilland DH4 biplanes. Unable to see service in the war, several were converted on the company's premises for passenger use with the installation of a cabin and two extra seats. They were painted white, as seen here, and used by No. 2 Communications Squadron, 86 Wing RAF, conveying cabinet ministers between London and Paris during the armistice negotiations.

The nursing staff at No. 9 Cedars Road, Clapham with a variety of kitchen utensils – kettle, colander, frying pan – ready to entertain the wounded troops being cared for at the nursing home. The notice to 'Take Cover' held by the boy scout is a reminder that they would cycle around the streets with a rattle to warn of approaching Zeppelins.

St Benedict's hospital, Church Lane, Tooting was used as a military hospital and many thousands were treated in the wards for their wounds. Five wards were badly damaged in 1944 when a V1 flying bomb crashed in nearby Freshwater Road. The YMCA erected the hut in the grounds of the hospital to provide a rest room and canteen for the soldiers. Private and commercial organisations supplied the rest room canteens up to 1921, when the government founded the Navy, Army, and Air Force Institutes (NAAFI).

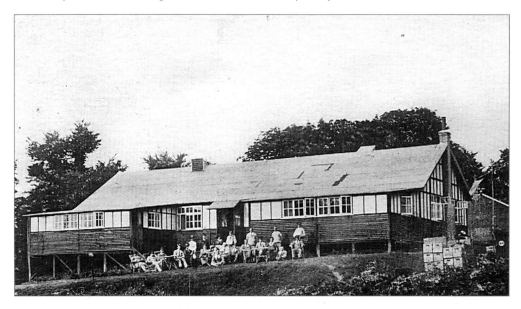

The Grove hospital, Blackshaw Road, Tooting was in use as an isolation hospital and as with most hospitals was inundated with the results of the slaughter on the fields of France and Belgium. The gentleman at his desk is a lieutenant-colonel in the Medical Corps and was probably the commanding officer of the hospital. The hospital was renamed St George's in 1954 and now forms a large complex on the site after the transfer of the medical school from central London in 1980.

Queen Mary's hospital, Roehampton Lane was opened on 28 June 1915 to administer to limbless servicemen. The wards were wooden huts erected in the gardens of Roehampton House and a limb-fitting centre was added. The men are seen relaxing in the canteen hut and also at the rear of the main house. They were issued with a blue uniform and a red tie.

After treatment, the men, wearing cap badges from many various regiments, await transport home. In the background are some of the timber wards at Queen Mary's hospital.

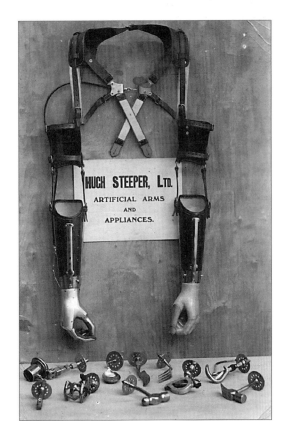

Implements that could be fitted and used with the false hands, 1920s. Hugh Steeper founded his company, alongside Queen Mary's hospital, in 1921 to manufacture false limbs and prostheses for limbless soldiers. The firm, still in operation, has been at the forefront of innovation to alleviate the suffering of those who have lost a limb.

The Royal Patriotic Asylum, Wandsworth Common, built in 1857 to house orphans of those killed in the Crimean War, was designated as the 3rd London General hospital from August 1914, specifically for the use of troops. Many lines of tents and wooden huts were erected in the grounds and on the common nearby, where as many as 1,800 were housed. In the background can be seen the central tower of Emanuel school, damaged in the Second World War when a bomb fell on the roof in March 1941.

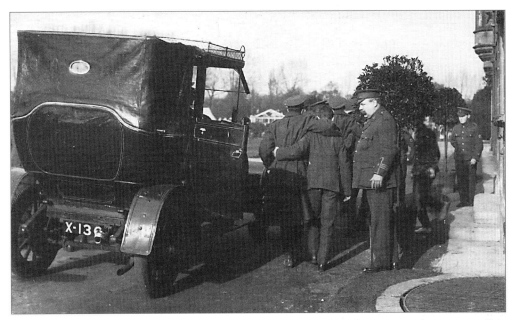

Patients were brought to the Royal Patriotic Asylum in an assortment of transport, where many willing hands were available to assist the injured.

In early 1918 five tanks were paraded through British towns to draw in funds for the war effort and Wandsworth was to see the tank *Iron Ration*. Displayed outside the Council House on East Hill, 12 to 13 March 1918, the tank was surrounded by troops, boy scouts, two bands and many curious onlookers. Sir Archibald Dawnay, Mayor of Wandsworth, climbed on to the tank to deliver a stirring speech encouraging the populace to give money. During this 'Tank Week' £221,480 was collected throughout the borough.

The Beasley family of Bolingbroke Walk, Battersea, 1917 or 1918. Each member of the family had a patriotic role to play in the war. Father was a private in the Medical Corps, mother and daughter were both in the Red Cross Voluntary Aid Detachment (VAD), the eldest son was in the Army Service Corps, while his brother was in the boy scouts.

The end of the First World War, in November 1918, was as much of a surprise as the beginning and the official peace celebrations were not held until after the signing of the Treaty of Versailles on 28 June 1919. The great victory procession was held in London on 21 July but local parades and celebrations took place on Saturday 19 July. The residents of Gay Street, Putney have tied an effigy of the German Kaiser into a chair, no doubt to be consumed later on a bonfire. The gent in the top hat might represent the USA, the person in white, the French, the man in the wig to the right of the 'Kaiser', Britain, while the 'bear' might represent Russia. The children were each presented with a victory mug and plate.

The Thornycroft lorries of Goodley and Sons, of 15 Replingham Road, Southfields are lined up by Southfields railway station on Saturday 19 July 1919. The procession paraded through the streets of Southfields, the lorries crowded with children dressed as pantomine or comic characters, seen below in Brookwood Road – one person on the back of one of the lorries is dressed as Charlie Chaplin.

Corporal C. Foster, a dustman from Tooting enlisted in the 13th Wandsworth Battalion, was awarded the Victoria Cross for his bravery in overwhelming an enemy machine gun position. To quote from the *London Gazette*, the official account, 'With reckless courage, he rushed forward and bombed the enemy, thereby recovering the gun. Then getting his two guns into action he killed the enemy gun team and captured their guns, thereby enabling the advance to continue successfully.' Below, Corporal Foster about to be addressed by King George V, when he and other medal winners were present at the opening of Southfields park on 28 July 1923. The park was renamed King George's park in honour of the royal visit. Corporal Foster, at 6 ft 2 in and given the inevitable nickname 'Tiny', was made up to inspector after the war and lived all his life in Tooting – he died in St James's hospital, Battersea in 1946.

The Furzedown allotment society, 1919, with spades and forks at hand in the grounds of what is now Graveney school, Welham Road, Streatham. Below are members of the Furzedown pig club, also 1919, by which time food shortages were severe, especially of meat. Rationing had been in force since 1917 and the council had to release much open land in 1918, for use as allotments, for food production.

Of all the many public crosses and memorials in Wandsworth and Battersea unveiled in honour of the many who died, only one included a statue. The Streatham war memorial, designed by Albert T. Toft, of a soldier resting on a reversed rifle – military sign of mourning – was unveiled on Saturday 14 October 1922 before a crowd of 5,000 and commemorated the 720 people of Streatham who gave their lives. Almost destroyed by a V1 flying bomb in 1944, the memorial was also dedicated in 1959 to the dead of 1939–45.

MUNICH TO SEPTEMBER 1939

The Prime Minister Neville Chamberlain flew to Munich on 15 September 1938 to meet the German Chancellor Herr Hitler and returned with a signed paper which proclaimed, 'the desire of our two peoples never to go to war with one another again'. Although cheered when he returned back to Heston aerodrome, many people at home and in the pubs were saying – 'Give it a year and we'll be at war with them'. The British government had issued guidelines to local authorities as early as 1936 on the need for air raid precautions. The government ordered the immediate distribution of gas masks on 28 September 1938 – a total of 35 million. Wandsworth Council had to find space to store and distribute 330,000 gas masks while Battersea handled 30,000. The mask on the right was for children and the model in the middle with two eye pieces and long breathing nozzle was issued to firemen and police forces. The others are standard issue to civilians, in a variety of containers including the well-known cardboard box, commonly seen suspended from a person's shoulder by a length of string.

West side, Clapham Common was transformed in 1938 when workmen appeared with picks and shovels to construct a number of air raid shelters. Of timber construction, they were meant only for use in an emergency by anyone caught out in the open. Only after the all-night raids of 1940 were the shelters rebuilt with a corrugated roof and covered with soil. Evidence of the improved shelters, covered with a tarmac topping can still be seen on the west side of Clapham Common.

The shelter, on the west side of Clapham Common, is ready for action, but being of plain wooden construction would not have proved very safe. Without a roof covering they quickly flooded.

The threat of invasion was intense and many blockhouses and strong points were erected on the outskirts of London. The Robin Hood roundabout on the A3 road, near Beverley Brook, had a concealed strong point built behind a garden wall and in this view a blockhouse has been built on Putney Bridge and disguised to blend in with All Saint's Church, Fulham. The sandbagged position by the trolleybus stop does not blend in so well. Naval personnel were stationed on all London bridges in case of attack by the Germans with naval mines. Any attack of this nature would have disrupted river traffic considerably; industry on the riverside included boat building, timber yards, cement factories, sugar refineries and gas works which required a large amount of coal delivered by colliers.

Several thousand Anderson shelters were erected throughout both boroughs, although slightly more in Wandsworth due to the greater number of gardens. The local papers throughout 1938–9 mentioned complaints from householders that their clothes line or fish pond would need moving. Mrs Beaumont of 11 Trentham Street, Southfields made a feature of their shelter – she added lumps of concrete to the earth-covering converting it into a rockery.

All road and rail routes were covered by a firing position, some built of brick and others of concrete. This small brick and concrete pillbox at the north end of the London underground railway bridge at Putney still survives.

The planned evacuation of children had led to the use of school buildings by the Auxiliary Fire Service (AFS) and the building of concrete dams to form emergency water tanks. Here the playground of Merton Road school, Southfields has been transformed with one of these dams.

Derek Vidler, aged 6 in September 1939, was under the impression that all males would have to march off to war. He and his brother, below right, are seen in the family garden at 46 Fernthorpe Road, Streatham digging for victory. Garden owners were encouraged to dispense with flowers and grow vegetables.

In a speech given in the summer of 1935 by Lord Londonderry, Secretary of State for Air, he stated that by 31 March 1937 the strength of the RAF would be increased by seventy-one extra squadrons, thirty-one extra airfields and the strength of the arm increased to 1,500 first line machines. In 1937 £1.5 billion was provided for expansion of all forces for the following five years. The keels of new battleships were laid – *King George V* and *The Prince of Wales*. In 1938 the Mayor of Wandsworth, Councillor W.C. Bonney, presided over the founding of an Air Defence Squadron for Wandsworth. Young men wait patiently in February 1939 to join the Air Defence Cadets of 34F Squadron (Balham & Tooting) based at Fircroft Road school, Tooting. By May the majority of cadets had received uniforms and the serious task of learning the skills of engineering, flight mechanics, flight rigging, wireless operating, photography and flying were keenly taken on.

Squadron Leader Edwin Brookes addressing some Air Defence Cadets at Fircroft Road school in 1939. The Air Defence Cadets were renamed the Air Training Corps in 1941.

Air Defence Cadets lined up outside Wandsworth town hall before going to the Empire Day air display at Biggin Hill, June 1939.

Cadets and officers of 34F Squadron on 13 July 1939 pose for a group photograph in front of Wandsworth town hall.

The dedication and presentation of new standards to 34F and the newly formed 82nd (Wandsworth) Squadron at King George's park by the Marshall of the RAF, Sir John Salmond, with the Mayor of Wandsworth, Councillor W.C. Bonney, attending.

The Bishop of Kingston dedicates the new standards, 13 July 1939. The flags incorporated the coat of arms of Wandsworth Borough, whose motto is 'We Serve'. Over the following six years the number of local squadrons increased to six and 1,832 served in the RAF and other services. Members of the Wandsworth wing were awarded five DFCs and one DFM, with thirty-nine making the supreme sacrifice.

AT WAR WITH GERMANY

Although the 11.15 a.m. broadcast on Sunday 3 September 1939 declared a state of war as from 11.00 a.m. that day, plans for the evacuation of children from large conurbations had been in place for many months. On Friday 1 September virtually all train services, buses and trams were commandeered to evacuate 400,000 children from London, with 22,000 teachers in control. The photograph shows mothers waiting to see away their offspring at Streatham railway station. The little girl is clutching her gas mask while the baby in the bonnet is pulling her name tag, tied to each child. William Mackett, aged 4¾ years, from Mantua Street, Battersea was evacuated to Spencers Wood, Reading. Evelyn Hunt of Wandsworth went to High Wycombe. The pupils of Furzedown school, Welham Road, Streatham ended up at Chichester. The pupils and staff of Putney County school for girls, Mayfield had to be at the school at 6 a.m. and then made the long walk to Southfields station. The list of items required for each Mayfield pupil would have proved difficult for an adult to carry, and some kind motorists did fill their cars with luggage and take the girls to the station. Mayfield school pupils went to Woking.

Members of the 52nd London (Wandsworth Gas Company) Battn. Home Guard in training. Starting with an armband for a uniform and a few rifles shared by the many as its equipment, it grew into a useful military unit.

The role of the Home Guard, originally formed in May 1940 as the Local Defence Volunteers and renamed by Winston Churchill in July 1940, was to protect against invasion. With so many men away in the forces, those considered too old or young for military service were asked to join their local units which were raised on a geographical basis, and also by some of the larger firms, such as railway companies, the post office and bus combines. Young & Co.'s brewery raised their own company of soldiers within the Wandsworth Home Guard while the Wandsworth Gas Co. was able to raise a separate battalion, the 52nd County of London (Wandgas) Battalion, seen here training within the confines of the gas works by Wandsworth bridge. Mock invasion exercises included guarding the pillboxes on Wandsworth bridge from the 'enemy' coming from Fulham.

Young boys would eagerly learn from men who had fought in the First World War and the thrill of dashing through London's darkened streets as a despatch rider was keenly taken up by lads of sixteen and seventeen. A despatch rider of B Company, Streatham Home Guard, Peter Derrick Willeringhaus, became the first Home Guard member to be mentioned in a despatch. He was named in the *London Gazette* for his gallantry during enemy action. He was delivering a despatch on the night of 18 October 1940 when a bomb fell alongside demolishing a public house and burying a number of people. He was thrown from his machine, which was wrecked, but he struggled on, despite his injuries, three-quarters of a mile to carry his despatch. He then collapsed, and had to be medically attended and was on the sick list for three weeks with the injuries he sustained. He was presented with a certificate of commendation on 19 November 1940 from command headquarters by the zone commander, Maj.-Gen. N.G. Anderson, in recognition of his gallantry and devotion to duty.

Members of the Home Guard took to the task with a sincere and serious sense of purpose. Initially badly equipped, mainly due to the losses of the BEF in France, the unit's professionalism was gradually recognised. Young & Co.'s brewery had enough staff remaining to raise a company of men within the Wandsworth Battalion. The brewery was a large enough site to have made a strong point either in siege or defence. The officers within the London area of command carried walking sticks as a sign of recognition and two in the front row (seated) have their canes with them.

The Royal Patriotic Asylum on Wandsworth Common was taken over by the security services as an internment camp for refugees who had escaped from Europe. Initially held in a holding camp elsewhere, any suspicious persons whose story needed further checking were taken to Wandsworth. This became a clearing house and interrogation centre where intended spies were found out. The 1950s BBC TV series *Spycatcher* told part of the story within these walls. Those spies that could not be turned around to work for the allied cause were tried and hanged either at Pentonville prison or at Wandsworth prison, just 200 yards across the common fron the Royal Patriotic Asylum. The photograph was taken early in the war, with the fencing not yet in position.

The men of A company 28th Battalion (Wandsworth), County of London Home Guard at the Broomhill Road headquarters. West Hill school can be seen in the background. Comparing this scene with that on page 37, the brewery has supplied a fair proportion of the strength of this battalion. The date of this photo is 22 October 1944 when the Home Guard was told to 'stand easy', their hard and worthwhile task almost complete. When at their peak strength in 1940–1, the Civil Defence forces in Wandsworth comprised 6,700 personnel, 40,000 fire guards and 16,000 Home Guard.

The magnificent London County Council (LCC) schools were used, with the absence of pupils and staff, mainly by the AFS. Volunteers had put their names forward during the emergency period of 1938 and the men and women dutifully appeared for service when war began. The gentleman standing alongside is a regular fireman from the London Fire Brigade (LFB) whose job was to train the willing civilians. The Dennis fire engine, supplied by the LFB is seen in late 1939 or early 1940, as the headlamp blackout masks have not yet been fitted. This is Merton Road school, Southfields, renamed Riversdale school.

Small cars were adapted to carry four stretchers which were transported quickly to the scene of any incident. The 'stretcher parties', as they were called, had to remove casualties ready for collection by ambulance. They also assisted with light rescue work, removing rubble and timber. The white disks on their chests denote they have received training in first aid techniques. The canvas bags contained their gas masks. Stretcher parties were renamed light rescue parties in 1943. This photo was taken in 1940–1, probably at a school in Wandsworth. Mr A.G. Roberts of Swaby Road, Earlsfield is seen in the centre.

The LCC depot at Kimber Road, Southfields converted a variety of vehicles into emergency ambulances, stretcher party transports and, as seen here, London taxis into mobile fire pump tenders. Alterations to the vehicle include a towing bracket for the water pump and the spare wheel transferred to the roof together with a rack for the ladder. The bodywork has been painted grey, with white outlining on the bumpers and mudguards to assist recognition in the blackout. There were weekly reports in the local papers of people being killed on the unlit roads and 1941 was to have the worst ever traffic accident record with 9,169 killed on Britain's roads.

A service at Huntingfield school, on the Dover House estate, Roehampton in late 1939 or early 1940, during which the Coventry-Climax water pump and members of the AFS were blessed. Before September 1940 the auxiliaries had plenty of spare time to fill the sandbags and mount them against the watch office. The two men on the extreme left are regular LFB firemen.

The AFS post at Huntingfield school (post No. E2T), with canvas shelters erected in the playground as garages for the two London taxis and a 1939 pattern Ford. Made here in Britain, the Fords were chosen from local hire fleets because of their larger engine capacity and pulling power. The tarpaulins were left over the radiators to keep the engines warm and during winter the engines were run up every hour to ensure a quick getaway during a call out.

The playground of Huntingfield school with a variety of vehicles requisitioned for use by the AFS. Below, a regular fireman with the Huntingfield school auxiliary crew on a standard service fire engine which has the blackout masks in place.

The gym equipment at Huntingfield school being put to good use by the volunteer auxiliary fire crew members. The public were quick to condemn the volunteers as war dodgers and time wasters but the constant drilling and exercises were put to good use in a very short time.

Craddock's garage, Roehampton Lane, with engineering and workshop facilities, was taken over by the AFS. Below, the LCC have converted a Fordson van for fire service which is standing at the entrance to Craddock's garage.

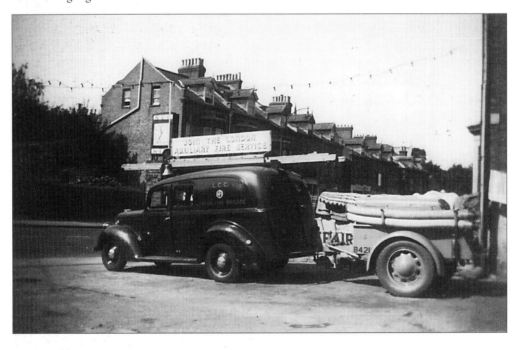

The crew at Craddock's garage keeping the Coventry-Climax water pump in good mechanical working order. The watch office entrance (below) is well protected by the sandbag blast wall and a comic among the team has painted and hung up a sign announcing 'The Snoop Inn'.

His Majesty King George VI inspecting a 3-inch mortar crew training on Putney Heath during 1940. The troops are from the Welsh Guards.

The AFS team at Hotham Road school, Putney (post No. E2U) had one of the youngest firewomen in Wandsworth, Mrs Kathleen Clayden, fourth from right. The Bedford vehicle is a heavy duty pumping unit supplied by the Home Office and designed for use in the war with the requirements for mobile fire pumps. The man is a regular of the LFB.

SOMEWHERE IN SOUTH LONDON

An early, local incident was the bombing of the Nelson public house on 8 September 1940, which stood on the corner of Nursery Street and Wandsworth Road almost opposite The Chase SW4. PC Edward Kerrison from Union Grove police station was quickly on the scene, where several people were trapped in the wreckage. He soon noticed, in the darkness, a partly clothed woman lying across a bath that was teetering over the bomb crater. As the woman struggled to release herself, the bath slipped ever closer to the crater and PC Kerrison forced himself up to the first floor and rescued the woman shortly before the bath plunged into the crater. Kerrison, a resident of Shamrock Road, Clapham was later awarded the recently instituted George Medal for his bravery – one of nineteen awarded for gallantry in the Borough of Wandsworth. PC Kerrison had also helped in rescuing a child and three women in another bombing incident where the premises were completely demolished. He already held the Distinguished Conduct Medal, Meritorious Service Medal, 1914 Star and the general service and victory medals of the previous war, serving as Company Sergeant Major in the Herts & Beds Light Infantry.

Clapham Junction railway station was bombed on several occasions throughout September, October and November 1940. Damaged rolling stock and uprooted rail lines are much in evidence in this scene. The railway repair gangs were upon the scene of any incident very quickly and disruption was always kept to a minimum. Battersea had a number of prime targets for the bombers – riverside industry, Battersea power station, the Projectile Engineering Co. works, Nine Elms gas works, two important rail river bridges and the vast railway yards of Nine Elms. However, local housing was to suffer far more damage than any of these strategic targets.

Due to the number of railway staff that had been absorbed into the fighting services, women were employed to take on duties previously seen as male-only occupations. Mrs Gunter and workmates, relaxing at the end of the war, were employed to clean locomotives and carriages at Clapham Junction and Nine Elms.

The Odeon cinema on Balham Hill, opened on 16 April 1938, took a direct hit in October 1940, demolishing the right half of the facade and the ground floor shop. The roof of the auditorium is camouflaged and a sandbagged look out position is exposed for everyone to see. In the scene below, the tram tracks have been torn up by another bomb but a portion of the roadway has already been cleared of rubble to allow other traffic to pass. Beyond the lamppost on the right, shored up by three massive wooden posts, is the tower containing the winding gear for the lift shaft used in the construction of the deep level shelter which became ready for use in 1942.

Air raid wardens' posts were sometimes set up within a concrete blockhouse – for very good reasons. The following sequence of photographs depict damage to a warden's post (No. L102 – Tel. Tulse Hill 5339) at the height of the blitz. The roundabout is at the junction of Atkin's Road, Thornton Road, Weir Road and Clarence Avenue, Clapham Park. Notice that all of the illuminated 'keep left' signs were removed as blackout precautions. The lamp standards have a 'barber's pole' paint finish and the kerbstones have red and white checkerboard markings. A bomb has fallen very close by and gouged out splinters of concrete from the camouflaged blockhouse.

Both houses facing the roundabout at Atkin's Road have been bomb blasted, losing the glass from windows, which in the upper view are boarded up, and tiles have been dislodged from every roof. The roadway and gardens are strewn with debris from the bomb and it appears that the gas mains or water supplies are being repaired.

The chapter heading 'Somewhere in South London' refers to newspaper reports which were heavily censored, but various clues sometimes provide useful information. The original caption to this photograph mentions 'Limbless ex-service men looking at a bomb crater at a hospital in the London area'. The high explosive bomb fell on 29 October 1940 near the huts where artificial limbs were manufactured at Queen Mary's hospital, Roehampton Lane.

In January 1941 a bomb fell at the junction of Christchurch Road and Brixton Hill, severely damaging the tram tracks. A specially laid single line of track was installed to bypass the crater. Each driver entering the single line was handed a 'token' which had to be passed to the driver of the tram coming back, ensuring that only one vehicle was on the track at any time hence avoiding a collision. The scene is by the Telford Avenue tram depot, Streatham High Road.

Barrage balloons were installed in many local parks, as here on Streatham Common; Immanuel Church can be seen in the background. Initially the balloons were manned by RAF personnel and later supplemented by members of the ATS. Several vehicles were attached to each unit, one to supply hydrogen gas, one for the winch and others for stores. Attached by a steel cable from a winch, the balloons were flown at a height of 5,000 to 6,000 ft to deter pilots and deflect bombers from accurate targeting. It was not unknown for the balloons to break free and one schoolgirl, Joan White of 12 Corunna Road, Battersea was frightened out of her wits. While in the outside lavatory one morning, she was disturbed by what she hesitantly told her mother was a giant elephant knocking at the door – Mum found out from the neighbours later that day it was an escaped balloon.

After a bombing raid on St John's Hill, Battersea in October 1940, London Transport staff have the task of relaying the tram tracks and reinstating the roadway. The Imperial cinema, on the right, has lost some of its glass frontage and notice boards. The immediate post-war scene below shows that much of the damage was not repaired for some years – the building beyond the trolleybus pole still has a temporary corrugated iron roof.

Prime Minister Winston Churchill visits the Nine Elms district in October 1940 after an aerial mine has exploded and damaged almost 1,000 properties in the area of Stewart's Road, not far from the projectile factory. The prime minister has no need for a squad of guards to escort him among the shocked and dazed public still clearing up after the raid. Aerial mines, or land-mines as they were sometimes called, were in fact naval mines fitted with an aerostatic fuse and dropped by parachute and had a tendency to explode in mid-air increasing the amount of blast damage.

A high explosive bomb on 29 October 1940 has demolished properties either side of St Ann's Hill, Wandsworth. Pieces of iron bedstead and recovered timber have been made into a barrier with a police notice attached, 'No Through Road'. Beyond the Star and Garter public house on the right, the upper floors of the adjoining shops have collapsed in the roadway and the upper gable end of the primary school, just past the lamppost, has fallen out. Beyond the mounds of rubble on the left is the Wandsworth Technical Institute.

Nos 265 and 267 Southcroft Road, Streatham after an air raid in September or October 1940. Householders had been warned to remove articles stored in the loft as they proved to be a fire risk during the fire bomb raids. Here a single, small bomb has torn into the roof and, on exploding has removed the tiles from the adjoining properties. The house numbers were marked on the fences to assist wardens at night-time in answering emergency calls and postmen if the houses needed to be boarded up. The terrace was repaired and is still in occupation.

Cavendish Road, Balham after an air raid at the height of the blitz, October or November 1940. The greengrocers of H. Ware and the neighbouring shoe repairers have taken the brunt of the blast, while the Prince of Wales public house appears to have only lost a few roof tiles. The notice on the shoe repairers advises, 'This business two doors along'. The tobacconist's A.G. Charge has a very temporary roof repair of tarred paper.

The importance and strength of the Anderson shelter is depicted in this scene of damaged properties in Wandsworth. Wandsworth Council photographed much of the bomb damage to assist in war reparation claims. The corrugated iron entrance to the shelter is in the centre with the bomb crater to the left beyond the fence post – the fence has disappeared. The blast has knocked out the window arches and not a pane of glass remains. A family member would have the task of carrying a small case into the shelter, containing important family documents such as birth and marriage certificates, mortgage documents and insurance policies. These would go with the family if they were diverted from bombed areas or when moving to alternative shelters.

Four high explosive bombs fell along Mitcham Road, Tooting on 5 November 1940. The funeral directors of Mr Knox at No. 82 Mitcham Road took a direct hit; he was killed outright, together with his wife Sarah Knox, his sister-in-law Mrs J. Knox and her invalid daughter, aged 34. Mr Knox was very fond of his fine team of horses and was despondent when motors came into vogue. He had also served on Wandsworth Council for a short while after the First World War. Three sons were away serving in the army, while another was a funeral director at Sutton.

Garratt Lane, Summerstown at the corner of Burmester Road after several high explosive bombs had fallen on 12 September 1940. A piano lies on top of the debris by Vernham's stores and a danger notice has been chalked on the side wall. The roof tiles in Burmester Road have been entirely displaced. The keep left signs on the traffic islands have blackout masks which diverted the light down towards the roadway. The lower scene is of the shops on the corner of Franche Court Road after the 12 September 1940 raid; thankfully no one was killed.

Sir Walter St John's school, High Street, Battersea was struck by a 500-lb high explosive bomb on 12 September 1940. The delayed action bomb was lodged in a cupboard in the headmaster's room and exploded three days later on 19 September destroying the Tennyson south wing built in 1915.

On the evening of 14 October 1940 a large high explosive bomb fell in Balham High Road, burying itself deep in the road surface, severing the gas and water mains and also dislodging the sewers. The bomb had penetrated the tube of the underground railway station where 500 people were sheltering from the raid. The rush of water overwhelmed those on the platform and sixty-five people were drowned in a sea of mud and gravel. The driver of a No. 88 bus had stopped when he saw the bomb fall, and suffering from concussion had gone to a nearby first aid post. The roadway was undermined by the gushing water and the empty bus slid slowly into the enlarged crater followed by the upper floors of the adjoining shops. The 1948 borough guide mentions sixty-eight as the total being killed.

The reinstatement of the underground railway and Balham High Road, together with the tramway, was not completed until March the following year. The tunnel had to be cleared out by teams of workmen coming up from Morden and removing rubble with railway wagons. All of this work took place during some of the most serious air raids over London.

Workmen clearing the track at Balham underground station to enable rubble and debris to be cleared from the platforms and stairways.

Communications were considered a legitimate target in war and the railways were included in the Luftwaffe bombing campaign because of their economic importance. Although aimed at specific targets, the bombs rarely found their mark, falling more by luck than intention on to any particular building. Wandsworth Common station on the Southern railway was hit on the night of 23 September 1940 – a night of heavy raids over London when the warning alert lasted from 7.41 p.m. until 5.55 a.m. the next morning. The rubble and debris is being taken to fill the wagons behind the steam engine waiting at the platform.

A delayed action bomb that fell on 21 October 1940, together with another bomb on warden's post No. C21, made a mess of the shopping parade in the Upper Richmond Road at the junction with West Hill, Wandsworth. The two men are from the Wandsworth Gas Co. and are attempting to repair the broken gas mains. The white crosses on the window panes were made of masking tape, applied to stop the glass from shattering into thousands of lethal fragments in a bomb blast.

The LCC tram shed at Clapham was hit by a high explosive bomb on 17 September 1940; the tram cars were almost all completely repaired and quickly returned to service. The depot was more seriously damaged when a V2 long-range rocket virtually demolished the building in January 1945.

The fire station on the corner of West Hill and Lebanon Gardens, Wandsworth, designated E22, was struck by an oil bomb (high explosive and petrol) on 16 November 1940, when several bombs were dropped in the area. The station was fully manned at the time, and six firemen were killed in the fire which followed (see opposite). The building was partially rebuilt and put back into action in 1942, but was demolished after the war and a new station opened in 1955. A small plaque, in a garden of remembrance, stands in front of the station and each November the six firemen are commemorated. A warden at post No. C18 in Vicarage Gardens, Manfred Road, was also killed during this raid.

Five coffins draped with the Union flag together with the men's helmets, belts and fireaxes on top, at rest in the church hall behind the fire station. Those firemen killed were: Andreazzi and Aust, despatch riders; Beard, Company Officer; Brum, Turner and Isaacs, firemen. Fireman Isaacs was Jewish and received his own ceremony, hence only five coffins are seen here.

The funeral cortège passes down West Hill, Wandsworth witnessed by a large number of the local population. The fire station stood opposite the tower of St Thomas's Church, seen in the background; on the right can be seen the offices of the *Wandsworth Borough News*, where the censor has obliterated the word 'Wandsworth'. The large glass frontage was covered by a wooden blast screen erected with the upper portion left open to allow some natural light through. The police station has a sandbag blast wall, seen beyond the first hearse, and a brick blast wall past the main entrance.

Firemen in our vicinity were to suffer greatly – on 17 October 1940 a bomb fell on the firemens' quarters, a house adjacent to the fire station in Mitcham Lane, Streatham, where the majority of the staff were trapped in the rest room. Rescue operations continued throughout the night, even while more bombs fell nearby. Canon Salmon opened the doors of the nearby church hall which was used by a mobile medical unit. Eleven AFS personnel were killed together with a seventy-year-old man. A mother and child had chosen to sleep in a car at a garage in Babbington Road, opposite the fire station, and her seven-month-old child, Peter Chumley, was killed. The mother was hurled into the road by the blast but escaped serious injury. Fourteen firemen were killed in Cavendish Road, Balham on 6 November 1940.

THINGUMABOBS & FIGHTING BACK

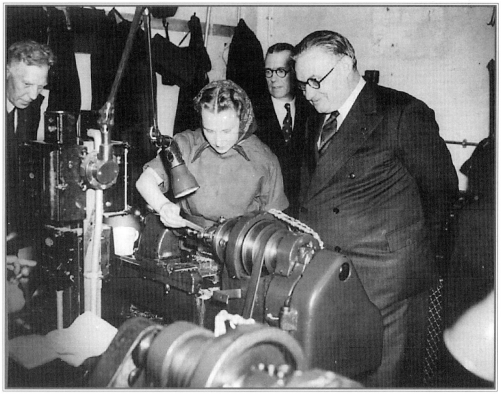

The Minister of Labour and National Service (a post ensuring labour was directed into war related work), Ernest Bevin, visited the Wandsworth Technical Institute, in the High Street, in 1941. The students were engaged in learning skills required in local industry and here a young lady is showing her knowledge of a metalworking lathe, no doubt later to make some of the 'thingumabobs' that Gracie Fields sang about. The college supplied specialist cutting tools, made on the premises during the war, to the large munitions manufacturer, the Projectile Engineering Co. of Battersea.

Mr Bevin shares a joke with the young ladies at the workbench during his 1941 visit to the Technical Institute.

Mr Bevin astride a motorbike in the mechanical department of the Technical Institute during his 1941 visit. The department taught students motor mechanics, engineering and the intricacies of the internal combustion engine.

Students line up for their 'life saving' cup of 'char' (tea) in the YMCA canteen at the Technical Institute in 1941. Below, women trainees collect their weekly wages.

In August 1940 the Mayor of Wandsworth, Councillor W.C. Bonney, set up a Spitfire fund with a target of £5,000, set by the government, for 'buying' a fighter aircraft for presentation by a community. Soon £14,540 had been collected which was deemed sufficient to buy three Spitfires. Spitfire Vc. MA281, 'Wandsworth-Clapham, Balham and Tooting Divisions', saw service in North Africa and Italy, before being struck off the serviceability list on 16 September 1944. Spitfire Va/Vb. W3766, 'Wandsworth-Putney, Roehampton and Southfields', was with 222 Sqn on 21 January 1943 based at Ayr, flying convoy patrols. The aircraft was transferred to 64 Sqn on 31 March 1943 also at Ayr, on convoy patrols and practising carrier landings on HMS *Argus*. The plane went south to Friston and Gravesend with 64 Sqn and passed on to 118 Sqn on 25 September 1943. It survived with 61 Operational Training Unit from 2 August 1944 until struck off charge on 10 May 1945. Spitfire Va/Vb. W3767, 'Wandsworth-Streatham and Central Divisions', was issued to 609 Sqn on 22 August 1941. 609 Sqn was the West Riding Auxiliary Squadron, based at Gravesend from July to September 1941 and moving to Biggin Hill some time in September. W3767 went missing on 17 September 1941 after only four weeks in service.

The 'Wandsworth-Clapham, Balham and Tooting' presentation Spitfire on active service with 43 Sqn, 'The Fighting Cocks', near Naples, Italy sometime between October 1943 and January 1944. Frank Wooley from Tooting is standing above the presentation panel giving a victory salute.

Warship Week in Wandsworth, 21 to 28 March 1942, was a resounding success with £1¼ million collected. Similar to the aircraft presentation scheme, the borough was able to adopt a ship and HMS *Cairo*, an anti-aircraft cruiser, was chosen. While on a Malta convoy, Operation Pedestal, that concluded with the famous incident of the oil tanker *Ohio*, HMS *Cairo* was torpedoed and due to the amount of damage had to be sunk by our own ships on 12 August 1942. Fortunately there were not too many casualties.

The Wandsworth Gas Co. had a large fleet of colliers that brought coal to the gas works at Wandsworth from northern ports. The collier *Wandle III* was struck by a torpedo from an E-boat on the night of 9 November 1942, but luckily did not sink. The captain and a volunteer crew saved the ship and it was taken in tow to Yarmouth where she is seen in dock below.

Morgan Crucible factory in Battersea Church Road, commonly called the 'plumbago' or just the 'plum', manufactured a host of materials vital to the war effort – in particular, carbon rods for searchlights and carbon brushes for electric motors. Many factories were put on to a twenty-four hour production schedule requiring a constant flow of workers through the gates, as seen here at Morgans at the change of shifts. Companies were directed to manufacture war related materials: the Slumberland bed factory at St Ann's Hill, Wandsworth made parachutes and P.B. Cows at Streatham High Road were turning out thousands of 'Mae West' life jackets, rubber dingies and barrage balloons.

The larger firms, such as the KLG spark plug factory on Roehampton Vale and here at Morgan Crucible, had their own company of Home Guard. After the disastrous experiences of the incendiary raids of 1940, all male employees between eighteen and sixty had to take turns as fire watchers on business premises. The bucket of sand and stirrup pump were seen at every building and many firms owe their continued existence to the well-retrieved incendiary.

An American Packard, converted at the LCC depot at Kimber Road, for use by the light rescue parties. The equipment on the roof comprises a ladder, four stretchers, several baulks of timber to shore up collapsing masonry and four wicker baskets to clear away debris, two galvanised buckets in the baskets complete the exterior equipment. Inside would be a basic first aid kit and picks, shovels and crowbars.

Admiral Sir Edward Evans, one of the regional commissioners for London, inspects stretcher parties and a mobile first aid unit at the municipal buildings in Wandsworth sometime between February 1941 and May 1942. These commissioners would have assumed full government powers for London if the government itself had been forced to evacuate in the event of invasion. Admiral Evans undertook the role of an 'outdoor commissioner' inspecting local authority Civil Defence services. It took over a year to inspect all 94 authorities making up the London Civil Defence region. A purpose-built Civil Defence training school was erected at the rear of the town hall. The four men in battledress are from a stretcher party. The man in the white helmet is a doctor. The woman in the white helmet is a member of a first aid post, possibly a doctor. The four ARP nurses are standing in front of a mobile hospital (a converted furniture removals van).

The countries of the world made efforts to alleviate the hardships of Britain and many canteens were donated. The Women's Voluntary Service (WVS) took charge of vehicles donated by our friends in such places as Ontario, Pennsylvania and Kenya. The Bedford OX mobile canteen, donated by the people of Kenya, is being inspected outside Battersea town hall. These mobile units were a welcome sight at the scene of a bombing incident where several hundred people could be involved in rescue operations amid clouds of brick dust. The regulars of the Telegraph Inn on Putney Heath collected £500 and presented an ambulance to the War Department in May 1941.

The Projectile Engineering Co. works occupied a large factory in Stewart's Road, Battersea manufacturing an enormous quantity of military shell cases and also producing vehicle chassis. Large areas of land surrounding the factory became available after the bombing raids and many remember the stacks of shell cases lined up waiting collection from the bomb-sites. The factory led a charmed life, for while all around were blasted to pieces, it only suffered a few broken windows. Small engineering workshops nearby supplied components to the firm and even the water board workshops at Kirtling Street, alongside Battersea power station, were 'tooled' up to produce shell casings.

The brick dump, off Stewart's Road, Battersea was to grow ever larger as the bombing campaign went on. As rubble was cleared from the streets of Battersea and elsewhere it was taken to cover the previously bombed and cleared area of Stockdale Road, Power Street and Porson Street. The 1946 film *Hue and Cry*, with Alister Sim, Jack Warner and a very youthful Harry Fowler, was largely made in the area of the brick dump and surrounding streets. The Dew Drop public house, Stewart's Road is the only survivor in this terrace of buildings, seen here about 1946.

The Home Guard together with the Civil Defence on a street exercise in October 1943 at the corner of Ascolon Street and Thessaly Road (formerly New Road). The public house is the Butcher's Arms and in Thessaly Road is Catherine Greene's hair salon, 'Madam Greene', and also Mr C.G. Joyce's bakery. To the right is a Battersea light rescue party van. Among the group on the corner is the Revd F.E. Worwood of St George's Church in nearby Battersea Park Road. The vicar was to be seen at all the local bombing incidents and many residents recall him dashing off somewhere on his bicycle to give what aid he could.

The bombed out streets off Stewart's Road and Thessaly Road were used by the army for street fighting training. The Devas Institute in Thessaly Road is where the Irish Guards instructors gave classroom lectures on this technique of modern warfare. The early model Covenanter tank of the Queen's Bays is finishing off the demolition begun by the Luftwaffe. The troops used live ammunition and a local boy, George May, about 10 years old, was tragically killed when he handled a live grenade. Extra fencing including barbed wire was erected around the training ground after this accident. After what the residents had suffered from bombing, to have the street warfare training area imposed on them was unnerving, especially after a V1 bomb exploded nearby on the Royal Oak public house and the army nonchalantly turned up for an exercise. The local women told the commanding officer in no uncertain terms that they were not welcome and the army withdrew. The exercises were intensified in the months leading up to D-Day, 6 June 1944 and the local population were warned to stay indoors or be unable to return if they were out. One young girl, Joan White, aged 13, trying to get back from school and worried that her mother, Minnie, would fear the worst had happened, persuaded the troops to lift the barrier.

The Castle public house, Putney Bridge Road was hit by a single high explosive bomb on 19 April 1941. The pub had only been rebuilt shortly before the war and the strong walls contained the blast, but the entire roof was brought down on to the crowded bars. The 1948 *Wandsworth Official Guide* gives forty-two as the number killed and 141 as injured, but the War Graves Commission list has thirty-five names. The discrepancy might be accounted for as casualties were not always dealt with in the immediate vicinity but could be taken to hospitals in Windsor or even Guildford.

Battersea Library, Lavender Hill in early 1941 after a bombing raid. The main roof has a temporary covering of tarred paper and wooden battens. The two top gables are missing as is all of the glass in the windows. The four brick blast walls on the pavement saved the basement from any damage. The posters on the wall urge, 'Fall in – The fire bomb firefighters', 'Use less water', 'How to tackle a firebomb' and 'Put out waste metal – it makes tanks, guns, ships'. In May 1944 Battersea Borough Council received a gift of £22 from Mr S.S. Conway of Bath towards the purchase of books for the reference library as a memorial to his brother who had studied in the reference library and was killed in an air raid on London in 1941.

Eltringham Street school, not far from Wandsworth bridge, with members of 89X AFS. The three men at centre are the regular LFB firemen. The industry along the Thames riverside and nearby housing was covered by this team, who had a close call in 1944 when a V2 rocket fell in nearby Petergate.

The Bellevue garage at 2–6 Althorpe Road, Wandsworth Common was designated post No. 181 London Auxiliary Ambulance Station (LAAS). The standard compliment of these stations was seven ambulances and five cars. Accommodation for the thirty-four staff was at 24 Bellvue Road. The magnificent vehicles here, including a London Ambulance Service Rolls Royce, are from post No. 180 LAAS based at Honeywell Road school, not far away, which as of 9 December 1942 had a staff of forty-seven with six part-time members. The vehicles have only one headlamp masked and the scene may have been photographed near the end of the war when emergency requirements were cut and shortly after the 1944 transfer of post No. 180 from Honeywell Road school to Althorpe Road.

Battersea Home Guard on Wandsworth Common with Emanuel school in the background. These could be senior boys of the school who chose not to be evacuated.

Lieutenant Colonel A. Liddiard, OBE, Commanding Officer of 29 County of London Battersea Battalion Home Guard, inspects the battalion on Clapham Common.

The Tooting Home Guard 30th County of London (COL) Battalion, lined up in Church Lane, opposite the parish church of St Nicholas, for inspection by the MP for Balham and Tooting, Lt.-Col. George Doland.

Soldiers will march that much better to a tune and many Home Guard units formed their own band – this is the band of the Roehampton Home Guard 27th COL Battalion. They were to appear at many local functions, including the sports day held at Queen Mary's hospital.

The Tooting Home Guard 30th COL Battalion in 1944. The headquarters was LLoyds Hall, now used by Boots chemist in Mitcham Road. The entrance was in Undine Street. The men are displaying part of their armoury – two machine guns and two mobile guns. Also on display are trophies won – the Battalion efficiency cup, Battalion miniature rifle cup and Battalion cricket cup. The men of Tooting Home Guard served on Tooting Bec Common with 187 Z Rocket Anti-Aircraft Battery.

The AFS team at Hotham Road school, Putney, post No. E2U. Two LFB staff are to the left of a despatch rider astride his motorcycle, centre. On the ground in front of the team are hose nozzles and standpipes for connecting to water board hydrants. A secondary AFS unit of Hotham Road school was based at 13 Malbrook Road, post No. E2U AUX.

The Mayor of Wandsworth, Councillor W.C. Bonney, fifth from right in front row, in the uniform of the town hall company, the Wandsworth Home Guard 28th COL Battalion. The man second left in the front row wears pilot's wings from the First World War and another has been awarded an MM. This is the main courtyard of the municipal buildings and the photo is dated late 1944. Nearly all the men sport four-year service chevrons on their right sleeves. Councillor W. Bonney, besides serving as mayor for the duration and serving on innumerable committees and saving schemes, was also the Commanding Officer of the Company and took part in all-night operations and exercises with the Battalion at Bisley and elsewhere. Born at Clapham in 1887 he was justifiably awarded the first honour of Freeman of Wandsworth on 10 May 1950.

The full complement of the Wandsworth Home Guard 28th COL Battalion on parade at Putney County school for girls, Mayfield, West Hill, Wandsworth, c. 1942. This photo was probably taken at the time when the Signal Corps took up occupation of the school, which was also used for training ATS girls. The school was seriously damaged by a parachute mine on 14 October 1940 and the top floor burnt out by incendiaries on 19 February 1944, the same night Whitelands college, a little further up West Hill, was hit. The playing field was ploughed up by a high explosive bomb on the following day and also suffered damage from a V1 flying bomb which fell on the corner of West Hill a little later. A list of incidents at only one school are enough to justify the evacuation of children.

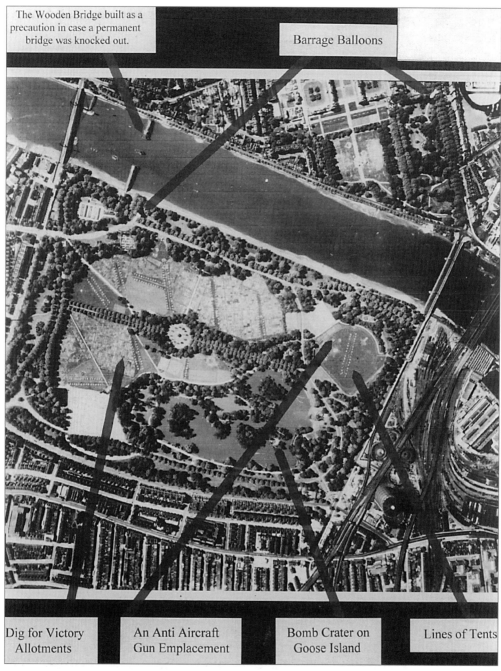

The Wooden Bridge built as a precaution in case a permanent bridge was knocked out.

Barrage Balloons

Dig for Victory Allotments

An Anti Aircraft Gun Emplacement

Bomb Crater on Goose Island

Lines of Tents

Battersea park as seen from the air in 1941, with north to the top. The grass gave way to allotments and army tents line nearly every pathway. The Royal Engineers' wooden bridge, downstream from the Albert bridge, was similar to the wooden bridge built at Lambeth for emergency use if the other bridges were damaged. To the right and slightly below the bandstand is a large white scar produced by a bomb blast.

The Standby Bridge
is complete

Anti Aircraft Rocket Battery

V1 Doodlebug Blast Damage

Allotments extended
from 1941

Pleasure Boats
on the Lake

Battersea park from the air in 1944. The emergency bridge is now complete. An anti-aircraft battery occupies the area to the east and the allotments have taken over far more land. Outside the park, to the left, the white scars of bomb damage can be seen in and around Juer Street and also Warriner Gardens. An average of seventy-seven staff were employed at Battersea park throughout the war.

The keeping of pigs within private gardens was not allowed but the wide open spaces of King George's park and Battersea park were deemed suitable. Pig clubs were encouraged as the animals did not consume food for human consumption. Bins were provided for food scraps and were carted down to the pig pens, as seen here at Battersea park – the pens were in the north-east of the park, where the tennis courts are now. Meat produced in this fashion saved transport costs and released space on shipping for munitions and of course supplemented the meagre diet imposed by rationing.

The bandstand in Battersea park was the stage for many fund-raising and patriotic gatherings. After the invasion of Russia by German forces in June 1941 the Russians became our allies and Mrs Haden Guest is seen giving a rousing speech during Anglo-Soviet week.

The Medium Mark 11A tank in Battersea park in 1942. This tank was used for training purposes and in the event of invasion would have been put into action, but probably more as a road block than as an offensive armament. Mr Edwin James, with large moustache, was a member of the Home Guard.

Mr Alexander of Bennerley Road, Battersea holding his prize cockerel. Many households kept a few chickens in their gardens as a method of augmenting the rations. If less than twenty chickens were kept the eggs did not have to go into the pool for market and could be retained. The egg ration in 1941 was two per person a week and the egg ration coupons could be exchanged for chicken meal or bran which was best mixed with potato into a mash for the chickens. Some families kept ducks, but when the inevitable time came, what had become the household pet proved difficult to consume.

William Pardoe suffered from polio and was rejected for military service. He is seen here digging his allotment in Battersea park, c. 1942. The soil in the park was far better for growing vegetables than the gravel found on Wimbledon and Clapham Commons which proved difficult to work. For almost 1,000 years they had been considered the 'wastes' of the manor. Householders living near railway lines would extend their gardens up on to the embankments, such as those behind the terraces in Gwynne Road, Battersea, and grow vegetables there too.

Mrs Fred Shaw sitting on the recently
dismantled park railings at Battersea park in
1942, before they were removed to make
munitions. The local authorities were given
powers to requisition gates and railings which
were soon being removed by gangs of men
wielding sledge-hammers, bolt-croppers and
oxy-acetylene cutting torches. Householders'
complaints flooded in because of the damage
caused to walls, steps and pathways. Railings
were retained for safety reasons on steep steps
or near basements and very rarely if the owner
objected or where historical associations had
to be considered. The cast-iron in railings was
of poor quality but was sorted into various
grades and melted down. The poorer quality
was used in castings where strength was not a
criterion and better grades were converted
into steel – very little was wasted. Great
damage was done to our heritage with the
cutting up of rare vehicles and melting down
of weapons captured in Victorian military
campaigns, but desperate measures were
needed to shore up our forces.

Wardens of C district, on the green at the junction of Holmbush Road and Rushholme Road, Putney. This
is early 1940 and before the blitz. Although all have been issued with helmets, few have been given
uniforms or service issue gas masks; the lady on the right has a civilian issue cardboard box container for
her gas mask.

The anti-aircraft unit on Clapham Common, manned by units of the Royal Artillery, started as a four-gun battery using 4.5-in guns and was increased to a six-gun battery with the Home Guard providing men for the two extra guns. The Commanding Officer was the archaeologist Sir Mortimer Wheeler. The battery unit designation was Clapham IAZ. S16. (Inner Artillery Zone. Site 16.) Anti-aircraft guns were also sited in Richmond park and on Wimbledon Common.

Queen Mary's hospital, Roehampton, 20 November 1941 (note the calendar on the workbench). The limb-fitting department was an important aspect of rehabilitation for limbless servicemen and civilians. The several limb manufacturers alongside the hospital were fully engaged in supplying many types of prosthesis. Prior to the use of penicillin later in the war, cases of gangrene often resulted in amputation.

Warden's post F47 on Wandsworth Common at the end of the war, 1944–5. Several ladies have five-year service chevrons on their sleeves.

A Battersea stretcher party, with almost everyone dressed for action. Each helmet has the letters S P, except for two with the letter T for telephone repair. The gentleman in the centre of the front row has his terrier dog sitting in his lap. The unit is unknown – unless a reader can help?

Furzedown school, Welham Road, Streatham was in use as a training school by the AFS. The lady with the peaked cap, in the middle of the front row, is one of the LFB instructors with a class of volunteers in 1943. In 1944 a mobile fire column was based at the school which comprised approximately 100 vehicles, fire engines, canteens, kitchens, wireless truck and petrol tankers ready at a moment's notice to go anywhere.

Battersea railway station, on the embankment above the High Street, was set alight during a raid on 21 October 1940. The station was never rebuilt and is seen here some years after the war, before it was demolished. This corner of the High Street and Gwynne Road is where the V1 flying bomb caused so much damage in 1944 (see page 127).

The boys of St George's school, Thessaly Road, Battersea were evacuated to Pembrokeshire in Wales. The potato was an important part of the wartime diet and the schoolboys were 'volunteered' to bring in the crop, a back-breaking task before the advent of mechanisation. The variety of food in the countryside might have seemed unusual to children from London. With luck, depending upon the family you were billeted with, rabbit and other game could be on the menu.

Pupils from Woodmansterne Road school, Streatham about to enter the gates of a village school in Carmarthen, Wales. All are carrying their gas masks. Some of these small village schools had to cope with different age groups of pupils in a single class, but this did not appear to cause too many problems. Villages would at times be overwhelmed by children from Birmingham and London; mixed together with the local children, this could cause rivalry and disputes.

Staff and pupils of Bolingbroke Walk school, Battersea in 1941. The school was the headquarters of G post wardens and members of staff and a few of the children are wearing Battersea ARP uniforms and badges. Many parents would not let their children be evacuated and ad hoc lessons had to be arranged, which were usually carried out in church halls. Many school buildings were to have strange inhabitants and uses during the war by units of ARP, AFS or ambulance crews. At Putney High school for girls, Putney Hill the police set up a parallel headquarters to Scotland Yard. Whitelands college, Southfields became a home for refugees from Gibraltar. Franciscan Road school, Tooting became a cotton store.

Battersea Civil Defence wardens used the bombed out ruins of Southlands college in Battersea High Street as a headquarters and training ground. In the background, to the right, is an emergency stockpile of coal. Wardens had to make a daily list of the full names and addresses of everyone within their district and also record any visitors, who legally had to register with the local wardens. This enabled the wardens to identify any victims of bombing and ensured time was not wasted in searching for someone who had left the area. The wardens were the first to report any incident and would call in the emergency services depending on the severity of destruction. The man on the far left of the front row (with W/FG on his helmet) had the duty of fire guard.

After vacating Mayfield school in 1942, the Wandsworth Home Guard 28th COL moved to Brandlehow Road school, off Putney Bridge Road. The group, now well armed with rifles, are on Sunday morning parade in 1943.

Brandlehow Road, Wandsworth was bombed on several occasions by high explosive bombs; at first a UXB detonated on 8 September 1940 and another fell on Nos 36 and 38 in the road on 10 May 1941. The school took a direct hit from a V1 flying bomb on 12 July 1944 which produced the results shown overleaf.

The upper view of Brandlehow Road school shows evidence of brickwork installed after the attack, possibly with the intention of reinstating the remains. Unfortunately the decision was made to demolish the school, as shown in these photographs taken in 1945. In the background can be seen the prefabs installed along Fawe Park Road.

The boys of Emanuel school, Wandsworth Common, while evacuated to Petersfield, Hampshire, manned their own company of Home Guard, seen here about 1943.

The blitz lasted from September 1940 to May 1941 and after this episode the population began to relax and get on with life. Small raids did take place, but in 1943 a new tactic developed; a lone aircraft would fly over looking for targets of opportunity. This photograph shows the 'Rego' tailors on the corner of Putney Bridge Road and Putney High Street in about 1935. By the beginning of the war the premises next-door but one, No. 35 High Street (off to the right of the picture) had become the Black and White milk bar, a popular meeting place, with the Cinderella dance club above. On the evening of Sunday 7 November 1943 both these venues were crowded with young people enjoying themselves.The two High Street cinemas were just emptying when a solitary 500-lb bomb was dropped from a roving aircraft and fell on to the roof of the dance-hall.

The dance-hall building suffered a total collapse and rubble and victims covered the roadway. Large, heavy rescue vehicles are being filled with debris and a crane on the left is lifting out large buckets of rubbish as rescue workers scramble over parts of the collapsed roof and flooring. The LCC heavy rescue service recommended awards to the following personnel: to Arthur James Rickman, the BEM; to Robert James Bonwell, George Edward Mills, Frank Thomas Cordery and Ernest John Pennicott the King's Commendation.

Admiral Sir Edward Evans, regional commissioner for London, attended the scene and is seen here conversing with members of the rescue teams in Putney High Street; the man is pointing towards the dance-hall. The Wandsworth Borough guide for 1948 stated that eighty-one were killed, but fifty-nine names are listed from the War Graves Commission. Hundreds suffered appalling injuries in what was unquestionably the worst wartime bombing incident in Wandsworth.

Putney High Street on 8 November 1943. Friends, relatives and survivors of the dance-hall bombing are being comforted by voluntary aid workers. The injured were taken to hospitals in Fulham as well as many south of the Thames, and keeping a record of who went to a particular aid post, hospital or in which ambulance had to be logged for future reference, which is being carried out in the incident van seen here.

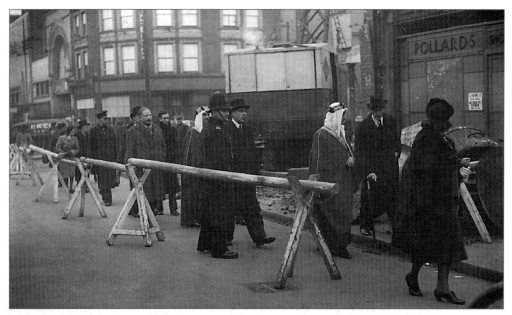

While the site of the dance-hall tragedy was being cleared, Prince Faisal and his half-brother Khalid of Saudi Arabia were on a visit to London and were shown the recent results of Nazi aggression. Prince Faisal became King of Saudi Arabia in 1964 and Khalid in 1975. The dance-hall site lay empty for over twenty years, perhaps as a sign of respect for the victims.

During 1938 the local authority inspected the basements of every shop to see if they were suitable to be converted into air raid shelters. Nearly 400 were chosen to have the floors strengthened and concrete poured on to the cellar floors, keeping them safe from damp. A group is singing to the tunes of an accordian, in the basement of the Bonbon sweetshop owned by George and Flo Sheehy at 420 Garratt Lane, between Skelbrook Street and Trewint Street, Earlsfield.

The timber strengthening beams for the shop floor above are prominent in both these scenes of the Bonbon sweetshop basement. Private photographs taken in wartime are unusual, but pictures inside shelters are extremely rare. Many shop owners today are grateful for the concrete floors laid in 1938 as they are in most cases still bone dry.

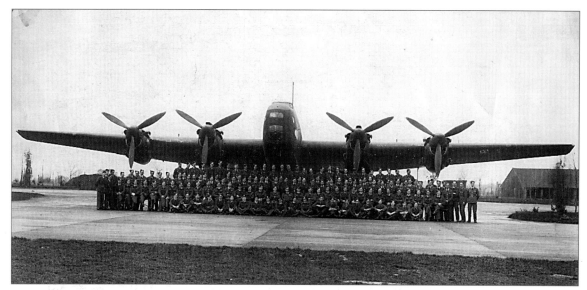

John Newberry, born in 1920 and living at 227 Mitcham Lane, Streatham was called up and served as an RAF pilot. He flew de Havilland Mosquitos and served in pathfinder and bomber squadrons. John is seated fourth from right in the second row in this view of his squadron under the imposing mass of a Handley Page bomber. John Newberry was awarded a DFC in 1944, 'For his bravery in pressing home repeated attacks in his Mosquito aircraft in support of the advance from El Alamein' (*Streatham News*). In uniform, at the end of the war, he sports the DFC, 1939–45 Star, Aircrew Europe Star, and Africa Star. Everyone had their part to play in the war and many men could proudly answer the question, 'What did you do in the war, dad?'

Admiral Sir Edward Evans of the Broke, regional commissioner for London, inspecting facilities at Wandsworth gas works with a party of government officials and military higher ranks. The date or reason for the visit is not known. Admiral Evans saw service in HMS *Broke* of the Dover patrol, which was involved in a famous naval engagement during the First World War, and Broke was often attached to his name.

Mr Wells giving pupils lessons in motor mechanics in the Civil Defence class at Wandsworth Technical Institute, 27 July 1943.

Mrs Duncan overseeing ATS girls (Auxiliary Territorial Service, the women's army) on touch-typing skills at Wandsworth Technical Institute, 29 July 1943.

Mr Ashton teaching army students the operating principles of diesel electric locomotives at Wandsworth Technical Institute on 16 August 1943.

Friday 3 September 1943 was declared a national day of prayer as the nation entered the fifth year of war. Students and staff of Wandsworth Technical Institute attend the church parade service, held in the quadrangle at the rear of the main block of the college.

The four deep level shelters along the Northern line of the underground railway were put into service during the flying bomb campaign that started in the second week of June 1944. The upper view is of the ventilator shaft and entrance to the Balham Hill shelter – compare with the view on page 49. Fold down bunks and beds were available, but were difficult to use when the shelters became crowded. The four shelters, at Balham Hill, Clapham Common, Clapham South and Clapham Road, accommodating 6,000 in each, were administered by the LCC from Balham Hill which had its own office, stores and printing press from where tickets were issued to use a numbered bed-bunk.

V WEAPONS TO V VICTORY

The invasion of Europe by allied forces had started on 6 June 1944 and many people had probably thought the war was now being fought far away. Although the government knew for some months of the threat of 'pilotless aircraft bombs', which were first dropped on East London on 13 June 1944, information was withheld from the general public by the censors. Rumours quickly spread as to what the explosions were, why the German bombs were crashing and exploding with such ferocity, and why no remains of any crew were ever found. The flying bomb campaign came to Streatham on 17 June 1944 when a V1 flying bomb fell on to the Empire cinema, which at the time was in use as an emergency food store. The bomb started a fire which proved difficult to extinguish. The railway line alongside was blocked with debris, but was soon cleared. One hundred and twenty people required temporary shelter as a result. Here, a policeman is guarding pieces of the flying bomb which were soon collected by an RAF intelligence team who were desperate to learn details about this new menace.

Battersea was also to have its first flying bomb the same day as Streatham's first, 17 June 1944. Later in the afternoon a flying bomb struck St John's Hill, wrecking the Surrey Hounds public house and demolishing neighbouring shops. Rescue teams were quickly on the scene and are pictured carrying a woman away from the collapsed shops on a stretcher.

The wrecked Surrey Hounds public house, St John's Hill, 17 June 1944. A bus was caught in the blast and was also showered by falling masonry causing more casualties. The pub and shops had to be demolished.

Prices' Candle factory, situated on the Thames river-front at Battersea, was struck by a flying bomb on 13 July 1944. The bomb demolished the factory's river frontage and set alight fuel oil and vats of oil used in the firm's processes. Barges moored on the Thames were ablaze and the river was said to be burning and barrels of whale oil and other oils from the factory were seen floating off on the tide. The fire service needed twenty-five appliances to control the blaze and two boiler engineers were discovered dead at the factory.

Hampton's furniture depository, alongside the Stewart's Lane railway yard and works at Battersea, was struck by a flying bomb on 31 July 1944, demolishing the upper two floors and spilling debris on to the railway tracks. Stewart's Road is to the right beyond the viaduct.

The deep level shelters on the Northern underground line were quickly put into operation with the arrival of the flying bombs. The lady on the far left in uniform is a shelter warden employed to manage the influx of people and to ensure orderly conduct while facilities below ground were being used. These included a canteen, seen here on 21 July 1944. The flying bombs were arriving at all times of the day and these shelters were occupied for almost the full eleven weeks of the campaign. With wireless sets blaring below ground it was suggested that the shelters be divided up between 'Swing fans and High brows.'

Streatham was hit by forty-one flying bombs, a high percentage of the 124 that fell on Wandsworth. Of Streatham's buildings, 860 were destroyed, 4,755 seriously damaged and 11,512 less seriously damaged. This amounted to 88 per cent of Streatham's total housing stock. A single flying bomb was known to have damaged 1,671 houses. The views are of the damage caused by a V1 that fell on to the front garden of 144 Moyser Road, Streatham before daybreak, 21 July 1944. The scene was of complete devastation, but thankfully casualties were light. The solitary house that has lost the back wall (above) stood in Furzedown Drive.

A householder of 140 Moyser Road, Streatham has taken up temporary residence in the garden shed after the V1 incident, 21 July 1944. Rescue parties arrived from several ARP posts and the Home Guard cooperated in the search for casualties. Admiral Sir Edward Evans visited the incident and, satisfied with the rescue work, signed the post incident log book and left. The Admiral sent a box of cigarettes to the wardens, which was much appreciated.

The residents of Pendle Road, Streatham were to experience the full consequences of the flying bomb when twelve were killed at about 3 a.m. on 3 August 1944. The bomb fell at the rear of the houses on top of the shelters from where the majority of casualties were recovered – a task not completed until 5 p.m. The Navy had released men to repair bombed properties and a squad nearby broke from their work and gave assistance in the rescue operation. Members of the WVS and Naval personnel are refreshed at a mobile canteen at Pendle Road. One elderly lady, made homeless and in her night clothes and munching a sandwich in the middle of the night at the canteen, enlivened spirits by proclaiming, 'Dear me, if I'd known I was going to a tea-party I'd have put my best frock on'.

When reports came in on 5 July 1944 that a V1 had fallen in the middle of Streatham High Road, the rescue teams rushing to the scene were expecting the worst. The flying bomb had struck some trees by the war memorial and exploded on the pavement nearby destroying a warden's post, a police box and shops. Tram drivers managed to stop in time and passengers were warned to duck to avoid any injuries. Fifty casualties were dealt with at the first aid post at Streatham baths and only one fatality was recorded. Both scenes depict the trams that continued running within fifteen minutes of the blast and the search for any casualties within the shops. A woman is being helped to the nearest first aid post.

Almost 3,000 houses were damaged and the resources of the Civil Defence forces stretched to the limit when three flying bombs fell within twenty-five minutes on the evening of Saturday 18 June 1944 on to Pathfield Road, Penrith Street and Downton Avenue, Streatham causing eleven fatalities. So many homes were left without cooking facilities that an LCC emergency meals service was set up in a local church hall. After the incident was deemed closed a warden stands by to assist in inquiries or to direct relatives, and mail, to temporary quarters, casualty stations or wherever.

This photograph is from a booklet produced by Battersea Borough Council in 1948 about the repair of war damage and is just captioned 'Flying bomb damage in Battersea'. What the photograph shows is the tremendous efforts being made by the rescue teams to clear rubble and timber away to extricate anyone trapped underneath. The V1 flying bomb, nicknamed the 'Doodlebug' by the British, carried a warhead of almost a ton of high explosive and could attain a speed of just over 400 mph. Thirty-six of these lethal weapons fell on the Borough of Battersea.

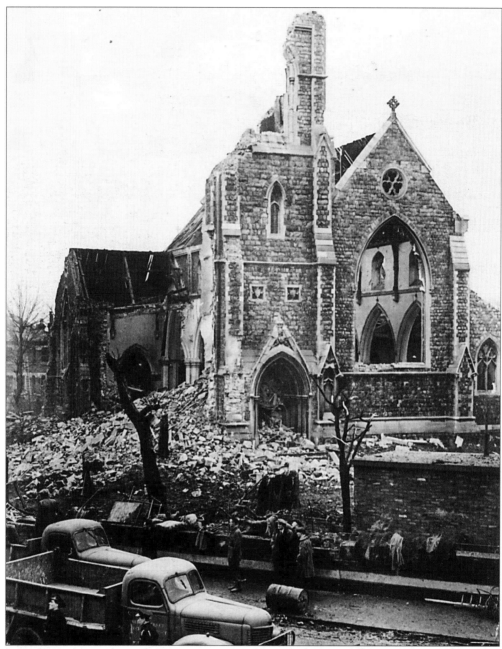

Whereas many of the V1 flying bombs were brought down by anti-aircraft fire or shot out of the sky by the RAF, no defence system could cope with the V2 rocket, which travelled at 3,000 mph and carried a warhead weighing almost a ton. Radar operators were not able, within the flight time of four minutes, to predict a landfall and give any warning. The first anyone knew was the enormous explosion followed a little while later by the sound of the rocket's 'whoosh' to earth. On Sunday 21 November 1944, in the Stewart's Road area, a strong thud was felt, shaking the ground, followed some seconds later by the sound of an explosion. This occurred over a mile away at Christchurch, Battersea Park Road. The force of the V2 brought down the church tower, and neighbouring shops and the fire station were severely damaged. The vicar's mother, living in the vicarage, was the only fatality.

Christchurch, Battersea Park Road, 21 November 1944. A mound of broken stone is all that remains of the tall tower and spire that had been a landmark since 1849. The church was demolished soon afterwards. In the foreground are the remains of the shops in Battersea Park Road. The trolley bus wires were brought down but the 'Princes Head' turning circle via Candahar Road and Cabul Road was soon back in action. This was the only V2 rocket to fall on Battersea, although one was shared in January 1945 with Wandsworth at Petergate, near York Road. Seven V2 rockets fell on Wandsworth.

The Mayor of Wandsworth, Councillor W.C. Bonney, takes the salute in November 1944 as the Wandsworth Home Guard march past the municipal buildings on their last parade. In the background is a brick water dam built in front of the town hall as an emergency water reserve and painted on the front is the commonly seen sign EWS – Emergency Water Supply.

The Mayor of Battersea, Councillor S. Fussey JP, shakes hands with Admiral Sir Edward Evans at the stand down parade of part-time services and the National Fire Service at Hyde Park on Sunday 18 March 1945. Mr Berry, town clerk of Battersea, is the gent in the Homburg hat.

Mr Winston Churchill announced on 7 May 1945 that the war in Europe was over and that the following day was to be considered VE-Day and that 'we could have a period of rejoicing'. Flags and bunting appeared everywhere and timber was taken from bomb-sites to stoke bonfires, some in the middle of streets, that burned all night. Mothers had been hoarding food items and ration cards in the certain knowledge that this day would arrive. Baking of cakes began almost immediately and committees of women pooled their resources ready for an explosion of joy. Most parties took place that Saturday, but others were delayed until June or even July. Here, the residents of Chatfield Road, off York Road, Battersea, enjoy their day; in the background is an impromptu stage constructed from scaffold poles.

The playground of Mendip Crescent flats, next to Chatfield Road, Battersea is the venue for the VE-Day party. The gas masks have been discarded for party masks.

Galveston Road, Wandsworth, victory party. Many of the menfolk were to stay in the forces until 1946 and in any victory party photograph, men are noticeably absent. The few on hand were either those wounded or prisoners of war that had been repatriated or had spent the war years in the Home Guard or as wardens. A bonfire has been piled high on the bomb-site; above on a scaffold is an effigy of Adolf Hitler, to be consumed when the bonfire is lit.

As the copy of the *News Chronicle*, lying on the empty chair announces, 'Japanese forces surrender'. VJ-Day was declared as 15 August 1945 and by 18 August the residents of Fernthorpe Road, Streatham were celebrating in style. In the background is a street shelter decorated with a large 'V'.

Queen Mary visited the street party at Latchmere Grove, Battersea held on 6 July 1945. The street shelters were painted red, white and blue and the street was covered with streamers and bunting. The Mayor, Councillor S. Fussey, and his wife Mrs S. Fussey are to the right. Queen Mary made a point of walking the full length of the Grove and walking back to speak to the children on the other side of the very long table where 210 were enjoying treats.

The Mayor and Mayoress of Battersea, fifth from right at the rear, attended the Broomwood Road party where Mrs S. Fussey was presented with a bouquet of tea roses by six-year-old Joyce Runacres. The party was held on Wandsworth Common owing to the traffic in Broomwood Road.

The Mayor of Battersea, Councillor S. Fussey, with the Revd E.R. Sowter attended the Oak Lodge school for the deaf, Nightingale Lane, during their celebrations on returning to the school building which had been damaged the previous year by a V1. The temporary home for the girls had been Springwell House, Clapham Common.

The residents of Bewick Street, Tennyson Street and Silverthorne Road, Battersea held their party at Tennyson Street school. About 100 children were entertained until 7.15 p.m. when each child was given a shilling and a bag of sweets. The adults then took over and 250 attended. Both parties were paid for with excess funds collected by wardens during the war in the event of any of them falling sick or suffering from enemy action.

During Warship Week in March 1942, the people of Battersea raised £½ million and adopted the destroyer HMS *Bulldog*. The ship had been through many actions – Dunkirk, the Norway campaign, convoys in the Arctic and Mediterranean, and taking part in the North African landings. The Battersea Borough flag was on board when the ship was involved in the surrender of the German garrison on the Channel Islands, 7 May 1945. Fifty of the ship's crew were fêted when they made a visit to Battersea in July 1945. The Mayor took the salute at the town hall, Lavender Hill before the crew were given lunch and tea at the Ardington Rooms, St John's Hill and the Granada cinema issued free tickets to the crew for that night's show.

Peace celebrations in Scholars Road, Balham. We can imagine the mothers saying to the youngsters, 'Sit, smile and be quiet – we don't have a chance to celebrate this kind of thing too often'. Mothers must have been pleased that her little 'Johnny' was not bringing home another prized piece of shrapnel or, as had happened at times, a live shell or bullet.

The ladies of Bolingbroke Walk, Battersea can relax and smile at the end of the war in 1945. The Home Front had been almost as dangerous as many battlefields, with many troops returning in 1946 expressing surprise at the disappearance of so many familiar buildings. The women had to struggle with the ration system; trying to concoct a meal from corned beef or a few scraps of meat was always a magician's trick. Rationing was not to end until 1954. In the background, in Battersea Church Road, is the Morgan Crucible factory.

The housing stock in Wandsworth and Battersea was in a dire state. Both boroughs were employing thousands of men to repair buildings and even British and American troops were helping with the enormous task. In Battersea 3,000 houses were demolished or considered a total loss and virtually every house had suffered damage; 22,000 had been repaired by 1948. Some properties needed multiple repairs during periods of severe bombing. In Wandsworth over 4,000 buildings had to be demolished and 72,000 were damaged. With such a chronic shortage of housing, many hundreds of prefabricated houses were located on cleared bomb-sites and also on Wandsworth and Clapham Commons. Here, on 29 January 1947 (during a bitter winter), the Minister of Works, Mr George Tomlinson, and the Mayor of Wandsworth attend the formal opening in Drakefield Road, Balham of the 100,000th temporary housing units erected since the start of the war. The new tenants Mr and Mrs J. Fenwick with their three children had been bombed out of their old home in 1944.

The prefabs in Queenstown Road, Battersea replaced Nos 321–7, which were demolished. Where the row of prefabs was in a line away from the road they would be given a suffix letter, i.e. 8, 8a, 8b. Patrick Loobey lived at 8a Atney Road, Putney for eleven years. The prefab introduced many families to the delights of a fridge, a washing machine or boiler and the convenience of running hot water and a separate bathroom – previous experience of those bombed out was commonly a copper to heat the water and a zinc bath to bathe in.

Christchurch, Battersea as it looked about 1912. The number of properties lost in the war refers to housing – mention of business premises, churches and places of entertainment was unusual and these were rarely replaced. Christchurch was built in 1849 and destroyed in 1944. The church gardens, laid out for public use in 1884, were re-dedicated to Battersea's war dead after the Second World War.

The Shakespeare Theatre, Lavender Hill, Battersea, built in 1896 and converted for cinema performances in 1923, was badly damaged by fire bombs in 1940. The building was left an empty shell, home to pigeons and inquisitive youngsters, until demolition in January 1957, when this interior scene was captured on film.

LONDON. Lavender Hill, Battersea. No. 1794.

The Pavilion cinema, Lavender Hill, Battersea is shown here in about 1925. It was opened in 1916 and destroyed on 17 August 1944 when a V1 fell into the roadway in front. The shops on the other side of the road were brought down and a total of twenty-eight people were killed. For several years after the war, a relative or friend of one of those killed left a wreath each anniversary on the wooden fence erected around the bomb-site of the Pavilion cinema.

Gwynne Road, Battersea, seen here about 1914 at the junction with Battersea High Street, was totally wrecked by a flying bomb in 1944. Besides the material and human damage inflicted, the bombing also wrecked people's lives as tight-knit communities, found especially in parts of Battersea, were torn from their roots and dispersed to the new blocks of flats erected after the war. Living in places that held no attractions and without life-long friends was upsetting to many thousands.

Opened as the Duchess Palace in 1899 and later renamed the Hippodrome, this 2,500-seat theatre, on the corner of Balham High Road and Yukon Road, seen here about 1914, was badly damaged by a bomb at the height of the blitz and was demolished immediately after the war.

Waldron Road school, Earlsfield c. 1914. This large and impressive LCC school, built in 1892, was destroyed by a direct hit from a high explosive bomb on the night of 17/18 October 1940. Several more books of this size could be printed containing nothing but lists of the buildings destroyed during the Second World War within the boroughs of Wandsworth and Battersea.